THE TWO MAJOR CITIES OF THE INCA EMPIRE: CUZCO AND MACHU PICCHU

HISTORY KIDS BOOKS

CHILDREN'S HISTORY BOOKS

BABY PROFESSOR

EDUCATION KIDS

Speedy Publishing LLC

40 E. Main St. #1156

Newark, DE 19711

www.speedypublishing.com

Copyright 2017

The Inca Empire, at its height, was the largest political structure in South America before the Europeans arrived. It had two great cities, Cuzco and Machu Picchu. Let's find out what these cities were like.

INCA EMPIRE

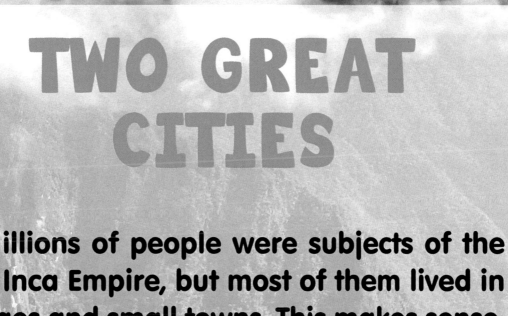

TWO GREAT CITIES

Millions of people were subjects of the Inca Empire, but most of them lived in villages and small towns. This makes sense, as most of the people were farmers and lived near their farms. However, the Inca Empire had a political capital (Cuzco) and a religious center (Machu Picchu), among other cities. The two cities looked different and served very different purposes.

CUZCO

Cuzco (or Cusco, or even Qosqo) is in the south-east of Peru, about eleven thousand feet high in the Andes Mountains. The Inca chose this place for their capital early in the time of their empire, in the thirteenth century. It remained the political center of the region until Spain conquered the Inca Empire.

INCA TERRACE RUINS IN MORAY, CUZCO, PERU

BURROWING OWL (ATHENE CUNICULARIA),
HUACACHINA, PERU

The name of the city is based on a phrase in the Quechua language, "qusqu wanka". This means "the rock of the owl." This refers to a myth about the beginnings of the Inca people, how one of the founding four brothers and four sisters first turned into an owl, then flew to where the city should be, and then turned into a rock.

Before the Inca arrived, the Killke culture had built a fortress on the site around 1100 CE. Before that building there were even older structures in the area.

KILLKE CULTURE

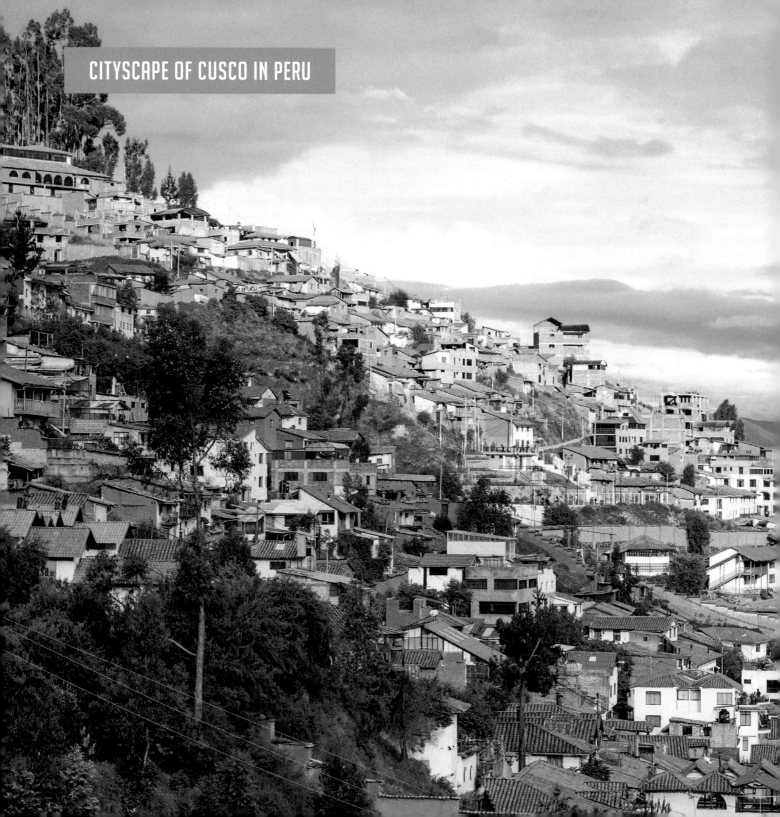

CITYSCAPE OF CUSCO IN PERU

Cuzco was carefully built: its structure reflected the Inca view of their world and their empire. They diverted two rivers to flow around the city, Cuzco was almost like a miniature world.

The city was divided in two halves, and each half had two areas. The four areas of the city represented the four provinces of the empire: Chinchasuyu, Antisuyu, Kuntisuyu, and Qullasuyu. A road from each area of the city ran out of Cuzco to connect it with its province.

The leaders of each province had to build a house in the part of Cuzco that represented their province, and had to live in that house for at least part of each year. When an Inca leader died, one of his sons inherited his title and the family as a whole inherited his property. The son who now had the title had to build a new house in Cuzco, and also had to help expand his province (and therefore the empire) so his family's land and power would continue to grow.

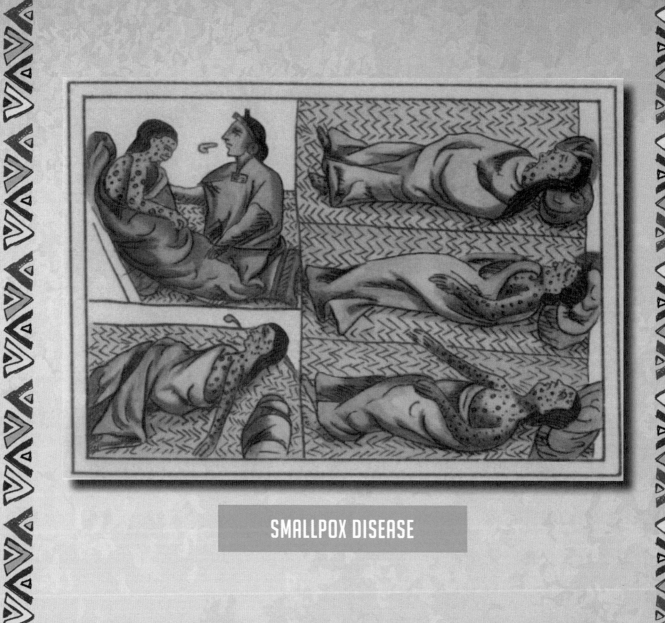

SMALLPOX DISEASE

In the 1520s the Inca Empire went through a civil war between two branches of the ruling family. In the middle of that struggle, diseases like smallpox and measles came into the empire, killing millions of people. These diseases came to the Americas with European explorers and adventurers, and the Native Americans had no immunity or resistance to them.

On the heels of the diseases came the Europeans themselves. They had gunpowder weapons, armor made of steel, and horses to ride on. The Inca army had never seen these things before, and faced them on foot, with weapons that were mainly spears and clubs. Although the Inca forces were much larger, the Spanish easily conquered Cuzco and the whole Inca Empire in 1533.

THE RUINS OF THE PALACE OF THE INCAS IN CHINCHERO, CUZCO, PERU

THINGS TO KNOW ABOUT CUZCO

The grandest buildings in Cuzco were the emperors' palaces. Each new emperor built a new palace for himself.

The bodies of the dead emperors were mummified and continued to "live" at their own palaces. Inca leaders would visit the mummies of dead emperors to get their opinions about what the empire should do.

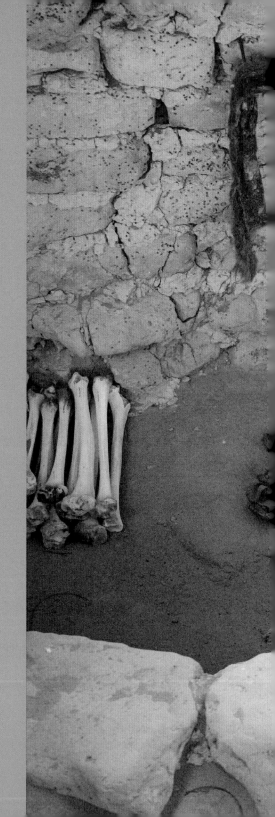

MUMMY

The Temple of the Sun was the most important temple in Cuzco. Its walls and floors were lined with gold sheets, so you can imagine how bright it was when the sun shone on it!

The Temple of the Sun had many buildings, with six of them assigned for worship of the six main gods in the Inca religion.

THE TEMPLE OF THE SUN OR "QORIKANCHA" IN CUSCO DURING INTI RAYMI (HENCE THE SOLAR DISC), PERU.

THE ARCHAEOLOGICAL SITE OF SACSAYHUAMAN IN CUSCO, PERU.

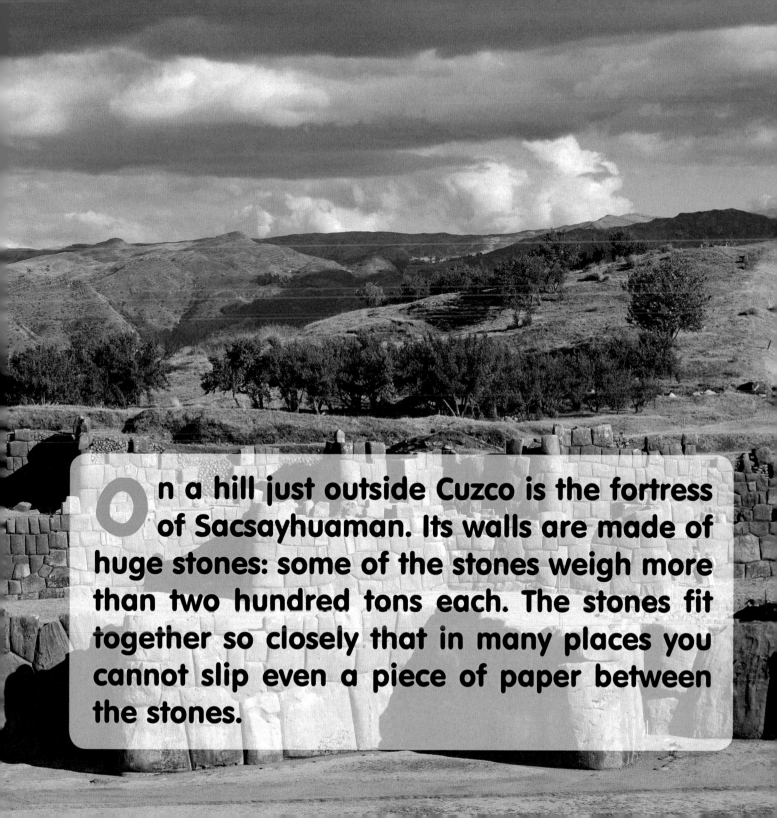

On a hill just outside Cuzco is the fortress of Sacsayhuaman. Its walls are made of huge stones: some of the stones weigh more than two hundred tons each. The stones fit together so closely that in many places you cannot slip even a piece of paper between the stones.

The key teachings of the Inca religion were "tell the truth, work hard, don't steal". That was also the phrase people said when they greeted each other.

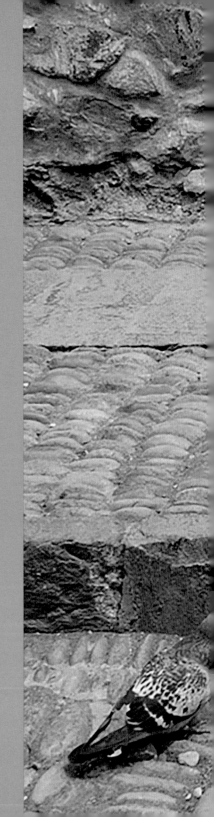

FRANCISCO PIZARRO

Francisco Pizarro, who conquered Cuzco for Spain, said that it was a beautiful city, and that if some of its buildings were moved to Spain, people would find them as lovely as even the finest Spanish buildings.

MACHU PICCHU

Machu Picchu is very different from Cuzco. While Cuzco was the center of power and was connected to all parts of the Inca Empire by the road system, Machu Picchu was hidden away to the northwest of Cuzco. Even the invading Spaniards did not learn of it, and it was only in 1911 that explorers found it again (although people in the area had known about it all along).

MACHU PICCHU (PERU, SOUTH AMERICA)

STONE WALLS AND STEPS AT MACHU PICCHU

Machu Picchu may have been a religious retreat center for the leaders of the Inca Empire. It is built on about five miles of steep land, with more than three thousand stone steps in the paths between its different areas.

Machu Picchu was probably built at the height of power of the Inca Empire, between about 1300 and 1400. It seems to have been abandoned after the Spanish had started their invasion and controlled much of the empire. It may be that so many of the residents of Machu Picchu died from the new diseases that its economy and culture collapsed and the survivors fled the area.

PALACE OF THE PRINCESS MACHU PICCHU

If it was a place mainly for use by the Inca rulers of the empire, then once they were defeated or killed there would have been nobody to use Machu Picchu any more!

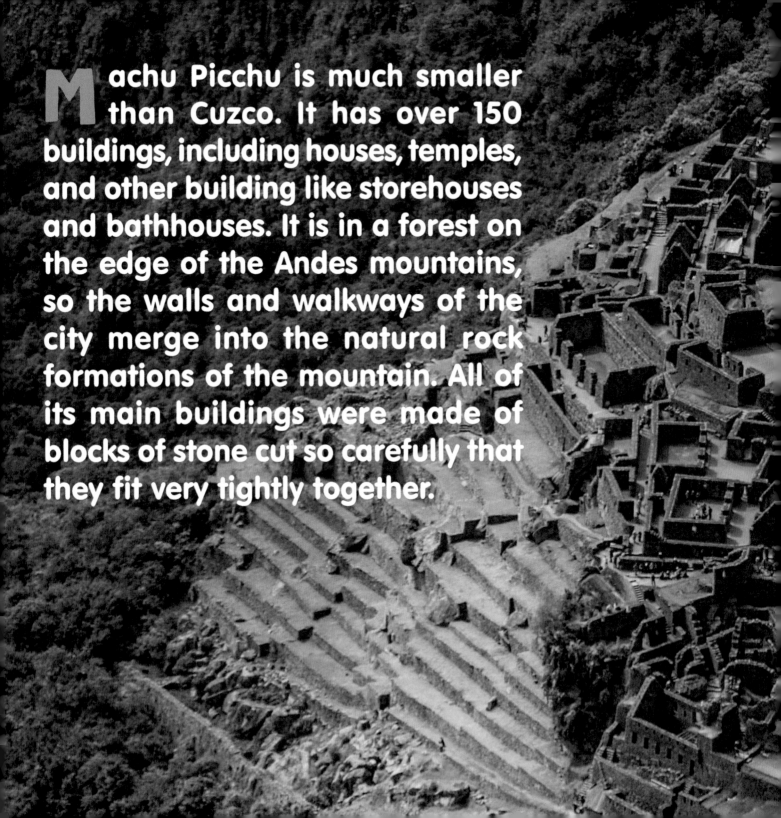

Machu Picchu is much smaller than Cuzco. It has over 150 buildings, including houses, temples, and other building like storehouses and bathhouses. It is in a forest on the edge of the Andes mountains, so the walls and walkways of the city merge into the natural rock formations of the mountain. All of its main buildings were made of blocks of stone cut so carefully that they fit very tightly together.

AERIAL VIEW OF MACHU PICCHU RUINS, PERU

THE SACRED ROCK IN THE LOST INCA CITY OF
MACHU PICCHU, PERU

The city had a worship area, palaces, a farming area, and an area where working people had places to live. There is a mysterious carved granite stone that may have been some sort of sacred calendar.

THINGS TO KNOW ABOUT MACHU PICCHU

Machu Picchu is about eight thousand feet above sea level, tucked in between mountains. It was not on a main route to anywhere else, so if you were not going to Machu Picchu on purpose you would have a hard time finding it.

When explorers found Machu Picchu in 1911, they were looking for a different "lost city".

HANDMADE CERAMIC POT

The explorers found and took away almost 40,000 rare and valuable objects, ranging from jewelry to statues, from pottery to mummies of past Inca rulers. The government of Peru fought for many years to regain control of these historic items, and most of them have now been returned to Peru.

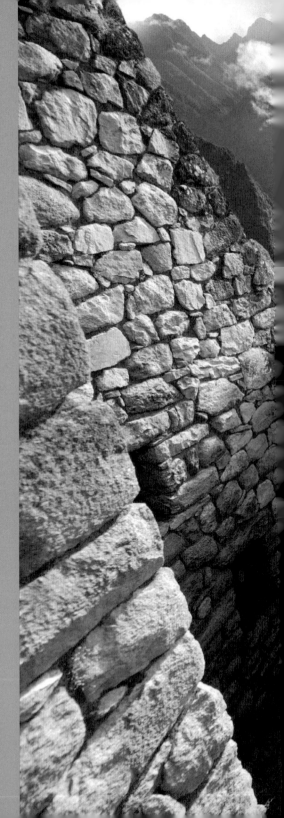

About one-third of Machu Picchu has been rebuilt to look as it would have been in the sixteenth century, so visitors can get a better sense of the place.

The buildings of Machu Picchu, made of dressed stone blocks that fit together tightly and smoothly, were designed to resist earthquake damage and other natural disasters.

WATER DRAINAGE AT MACHU PICCHU

When the Inca Empire built Machu Picchu, about two-thirds of what they did was underground. They built drainage ditches to guide water away from the buildings, and deep foundations to support the huge blocks that make up the walls of the structures.

Nobody really knows how the Inca workers were able to move all those blocks of stone and raise them into position so precisely. They had no animals like oxen or horses to pull heavy loads, and they had no complicated machinery for cutting and lifting stone blocks. Most of the work was probably done by hundreds or even thousands of laborers using their muscles. They may have constructed rollers made of logs to help move the stones along, but even with that aid the effort must have been incredible.

AGRICULTURE TERRACES

There are good water sources around Machu Picchu and much land that is appropriate for growing food. There were terraced areas, where parts of the mountain side were cut away to create a series of narrow fields up the steep slope.

Machu Picchu could probably produced enough food to support a population four times the number of people who actually lived there.

VARIETIES OF CORN

THE INCA TRAIL, MACHU PICCHU

If you travel by foot from Cuzco to Machu Picchu, along the old Inca road, the trip will take you almost three days over mountainous terrain.

MEET THE INCA

Cuzco and Machu Picchu show the remarkable abilities of the Inca Empire. Read more about them in Baby Professor books like The History of the Inca Empire and Inca Government and Society.

Visit

BABY PROFESSOR
EDUCATION KIDS

www.BabyProfessorBooks.com

to download Free Baby Professor eBooks
and view our catalog of new and exciting
Children's Books